THE BRIDGE

ALSO BY MARY AUSTIN SPEAKER

Ceremony

20 Love Poems for 10 Months

THE BRIDGE

Mary Austin Speaker

SHEARSMAN BOOKS

First published in the United Kingdom in 2016 by
Shearsman Books
50 Westons Hill Drive
Emersons Green
BRISTOL
BS16 7DF

Shearsman Books Ltd Registered Office
30–31 St. James Place, Mangotsfield, Bristol BS16 9JB
(this address not for correspondence)

www.shearsman.com

ISBN 978-1-84861-467-3

Cover artwork & book design by Mary Austin Speaker

CONTENTS

I wrote this book in the months preceding my
departure from New York after many years
of living in that city. Each of the poems was
composed on the subway while riding over the
Manhattan Bridge. Because I worked in Manhattan
and lived in Brooklyn, I rode across the bridge
twice a day. I wrote a poem each time I crossed
it for several months. This book represents a
selection of those poems.

Women on trains
have a life that is
exactly livable
the precision of days flashing past
no intervention allowed
shapes of each season
relentlessly carved in the land.
AUDRE LORDE

And so
of cities you bespeak
subways, rivered under streets
and rivers. . . . In the car
the overtone of motion
underground, the monotone
of motion is the sound
of other faces, also underground—
HART CRANE

The bridge *gathers*
MARTIN HEIDEGGER

for the train riders

THE BRIDGE

every morning going over the bridge
everybody going in to work
and me as well and me as well
as watching the lit up rocket
take off in the subway
someone named Bill left it there
so we could see what it would be like
to be that rocket
a cartoon is a drawing of an idea
on the bridge I have one foot
in Brooklyn the other in the city
it's the only time I can see for miles
all rippled by some sleeper's head grease
through this window on exhaustion
there are women on bicycles
with helmets protecting
their delicate heads
the train stalls
and we are at the edge
of the city of tomorrow
and now we are driving right in
to the city of right now
the paint on the bridge
is the blue white of milk
at 8:40 AM

there is a woman in a trench coat

whose collar wraps gently around her

shoulders she is gasping

having been told a word or two

I thought they were speaking German

but they are only

speaking English

and the signs in Chinatown are all Chinese

except the numbers

I have projected again

these person-sized places

under the bridge as though

I could sleep there

everybody going over the bridge

everybody going into work

and me as well and me as well

all land is no man's land
all bridges are erected
Miami is the color orange
therefore all cities
look like Miami sometimes
the warm body
of the polish *pani*
chatting with her husband
on the subway
is secretly comforting
the way the red clouds
at 6:38 PM are uncomforting
we never want
the same thing twice
because we are never
the same thing twice
symmetry is a pattern
more alien than
the sci-fi heads of ferns
alien forms are the oldest ones
trilobites shrimp
all ocean creatures
defeathered birds
transparent bodies
we have gotten more other

as we paled and colored
and multiplied in Miami
prehistoric ferns grow
beside lagoons with honest
to god dinosaurs
let's start with a simple fear
and stay there
what keeps me up
is the horror of being
human mistakes the way
time won't stop moving
control power removed
from our bodies
all land is no man's land
all bridges are erected

motion is never only in one direction
we roll in limbs flashing
static lighting up our dust mites
if ascent is only a way
toward another opening
then I am ascending
to my desk and burrowing
through the pages in a fluid motion
being a machine is exhausting
spending all the fuel each day
on the B train a woman
whose head is bent toward the ground
eats an apple and threatens
anyone between her body and the door
you must not be behind me, she says,
or maybe you'll lose your life
I do not own anything
but I hold everything I have
loss is sublime in its twin-faced
pleasure and pain
pure blank of scarcity
or the always almost last
lifting of the body
out of the warm salt bath of death
oblivion quiet as a snowstorm

or a night full of rain

snow drifts up rain bounces back

motion is never only in one direction

every evening all the people
going home from work
the light having run
a fuller race from
the day before
there is a grace
to evening's
colored ends
a settling down
as though we are watching
the dust settle on the day
which I have chewed up like a pill
at 6:37 PM
the watchtower's glass eyes
on the lookout for a final end
so there will be one
to the story she tells
to her millions of people
she is looking at the city
with thousands of eyes
waiting for the clouds to break
like an egg
full of blood
and the rivers to roil
beneath the bridge

its rivulets colder
than the day before
the fish put on their clothes
the people are dressed
in darkness by seven
every evening all the people
going home from work

to awaken to astonishing
geometry is to pull
our bodies from the bed
and from horizon roll
into anarchic day
bouquet of noise
and substance radiating out
our temperatures and breath
each temporary guess
the beautiful woman driving
the sanitation department truck
files her nails at a stoplight
files her nails in a ray of morning
sun the honey-scented flowers
are dying on their vine
and yesterday
the rain came down so hard
the streets were green for hours
the leaves so flat and wet
that we awoke
to an astonishing geometry
to pull our bodies from the bed

rain on the spiny architecture
of the bridge I trust
more than the blur-edged sunset
garish as a painted backdrop
today it took four minutes
red minutes left
unspooling over and overspent
to be carried over a bridge at 8:41 PM
into the shiny inviolate rain
is to sail on a manageable ocean
is an effortless walk in a quarry of salt
what happened today?
to ride across a wet black bridge
is to forget each item of news
and replace each one
with the spiny architecture
of the bridge

the bridge arcs over water
a protracted yawn a sigh
inspired expired never held
century in
century out
the water blows
its breath beneath
its drifts of no
and yes just past
its western port
green domes red edifice
the crayon box of Chinatown
rat caves branching
one half of the rising
falling ballooning settling
bridge an arc over water
a protracted yawn a sigh

we are moving into a sky
the color of doves the color
of steel and rivers and concrete
it is 9:18 AM and the sky
is pretending to be dawn
drawing the clouds over its buildings
like a sheet to shut out the day
we should shout or sing out
what we want all the way
over the bridge
while we launch
into air
on the back
of a steel horse
across the bridge
the N train carries
its dark bodies in secret
and when the B train blurs by
from the end of the bridge
everything is sped up time
we have lost again
in the blur
of watching the future
rush headlong
toward us

this is a kind of shelter this
horse launching us into the sky
the color of doves the color of steel

also plums
unripe and the bark
of buildings
how all windows reflect
on the expiring day
a man on a bicycle
water taxi frothing
a long slow S
into the east
river the sky at 6:18 PM
is the color of mistakes
oil spills bruises
translucent and borderless
also plums
unripe and blank

in the city of no memory
a ride across the bridge
in a sharp black wind
affordably thrills
when we have gathered
enough of us together
the buildings squat
hulking up the bank
as far as we know
sometimes the ocean
grazes our cheeks
a congress of fishes
from that very ocean
is eaten beneath these roofs
before going to bed
before waking up
to the anything-is-possible day
in the city of no memory

all of us trembling across the bridge
all of us red black yellow blue
at once two trains pass one another
as the buildings telescope themselves
over the city super heroes
of diurnal wretchedness
it's 7:44 PM and the city
is black red yellow
and we are entering the ground
where we live and it is only black
and blue all of us trembling
across the bridge

the air is an agreement
red sounds white
blackyellow songs
in the blackblue city
Manhattan lies down
with her head
in the oystershell sand
and Brooklyn reaches
her redyellow sighs
everywhere we look
every direction
we do keep coming back here
in a tunnel of white
percussive light
the air is an agreement
a sound a song

we are the people
of your neighborhood
and we are singing
and celebrating ourselves
across the bridge
as we sing and celebrate
the bright blue morning
sky of early fall
the cars along
the bridge are stalled
in the upstairs room
and the watchtower
looks and the bridge
stands with her two
feet in cold water
and the bridge is wearing
orange today
and paintings lace
her ribs and now
the people of your
neighborhood are
yawned right in

above the winking

red black yellow blue

a sea of rooms

lamp-lit distracted

it is 6:59 PM

and the moon

is a white coin

drawing the river to her

boats and their fancy dresses

the billboards in blankness

the buildings in quiet

and fall has fallen

these are the year's

darker hours

that we are moving through

above the sea of rooms

above the winking redblackyellow

and the redblack

yellowing blue

inside the tunnel's open throat

the sodium lights

address the air

a red bright signal

pulses from the bridge

a figure with his arms held up

we hold ourselves

across the bridge

and do not stop

for signal lights

or windows bright

with halogen

even the neon

geometric shapes

on top of buildings otherwise

an architectural mistake

not rain not snow

nor dark of night

will stop us

from the next

ballooning and

outrageous show

of sodium lights

inside the tunnel's open throat

we undertake

this fusilage

into the sky

by way of brick

and mortar

steel beams

and a blue

true dream

of sky

because everything

is happening

we excavate

our industry

to make more room

for those who are

already at the door

the sky is clean today

a single fog

that offers windows

twice as bright

as yesterday

more light

than we expected

so today

we undertake
to fusilage
into the sky

gone slack
a shrug
at once
the hustle
is only
sometimes
and so
we see
the train
all lit up like
a summer sky
a shouldering
gone slack

on the outskirts
of the morning
fog steel sky
brightening
the auditory
we're all picked
flowers nodding
our slender necks
in all directions
because the clouds
diffuse the light
like a silk stocking
widens the aperture
make it smaller
and the room inverts
it's possible to be still
between fits of sleep
and in the hour
after the alarm
when the light
sprays in
like a far away wave
on the outskirts of morning

the drama of crossing
the bridge is amplified
by the relentless
pop song forged
like a righteous hymn
we travel through
cacophony of song
bits and slow
groanings of machines
each of us mysterious
to ourselves
our bodies tick
their way across
the bridge and back
the secret public
shame of trying
for the last seat
on the train
all of us shabby
predators looking
for a break
to ride with rest
as a companion
is to fall in with
the drama of the bridge

and now it's night

the other train

a lit-up stage

parading the tired

at 8:43 PM two girls

gossip in Chinese

their dear dark hair

in strings around their

teenage faces my hands

are full of papercuts

from *Spain* I leave

a little of myself

in every book

such generous

letterforms

careful serifs

the smooth

of well-made paper

will always offer

the most touchable glamour

I like it closer

than the night's

ten thousand eyes

dressing her buildings

like a skin

of glittering stones
like a darkened forge
like a closing cloak
that offers itself
every day
but this evening closes
over us
curtain on a stage
with spotlight trained
on all of us
poor workers
running late
at 8:43 PM
of a twelve-hour day
and now it's night

and so

we bravely go

upward again

into the day

boats shooting forth

their wake

small cars

and smaller people

born for this

encountering

repetitive day

we forge

our difference

from the way

we on the subway

stand in testament

to everything

being okay

for now

all still

a frozen piece

of day

if we all had

a louder instrument

to play

then we could know
who had more days
to bravely go

and all of us in thrall
of greed sex safety sleep
in late October's warmer air
mosquitos copulating in
the rain-soaked leaves
we want the dessicating wave
of winter to embrace us
like a sky so full of snow
we watch each hour effervesce
and whitely wring
all color from the sky
how bare the land
the indian summer lays
above the river like a shawl
of finely textured skin at 6:15
so the tower is river is sky
is indian fall and all
of us in thrall and all
of us in thrall

yellow streaks
in the lit-up dark
and then the shock
of bluewhite day
and yellow cabs
a line of pink
a memory
of orange dawn
to stop before
one single frame
is to never go
entirely across
the bridge
to see between
its ribs
the yellow trees
raise up their arms
to Chinese roofs
the schoolbus starts
awnings yawn forth
giant spools of cable
for the giant holes
that someone fixes
every bluewhite day

in the zoetrope of white

and yellow streaks

in the lit-up dark

The river burns
her bright waves up
small offerings
to air through which
we plunge and Chinatown
holds her fishes and chives and small
soft-bodied fruits and frogs
enthralled in tepid buckets
paused in the interstice
between land and sea instead
with doorknobs rulers
and afterward we
leap into the coldblack night
of winter and the river burns
her bright waves up

the street already dark
the pier in its suit of light
rocking horse arcing
into the river as the train
across the bridge blurs by
an afterthought
as though we spoke each day
to one another
the train pauses
to allow us to regard
our own closed mouths
offers its lap and elbows
and a panoramic view
so we can see
how we are being held away
from a wild plunge
in a suit of light
into the street
already dark

all the animals come out

each morning

to walk the streets

is to exist

make noise

squint at the glare

from the sun-bleached bridge

it is 9:28 AM

and the other bridge

is blue and grey

and steam puffs from

the electric plant

its other form of water

as the river plods her course

light slanting on the buildings

as though they had

been dipped in cream

and then forgot

in every man

there is a monster

yawning

with thumbs in pockets

a child

with a hat full of sherbet

colors coughing and the gum

of a thousand nervous people
pocks the platform at Grand street
where a mall stretches back
to the bridge on this
midmorning nod
between frames of dreams
and the frames of others
these trains flash off and on
these others we could be
or be with all
those necks exposed
heads nodding down
all tender
undersides of ears
offering themselves
for recognition
we're animals
when we sleep
and when we barely
waking sway
each morning all
our animals come out
and then they go back in

A fog burns off
into the kind of sky
that hugs the coast
rain-wet shallow
scalloped like the scales
of bluefish marlin
belly of the ray
cloud-white
evenly we roll
over this
economy of fishes
where the dead
now dissipate
their thousand shapes
each one a wave
that reaches up
and burns off
into fog

winter radiates us forth
past a shotgun sun that grins
its early departure
over a green colossus
and her fleet of progress
that noses a steel sky
a coat of ocean
tongues its blue
green over the roofs
so the yellow shot of gold
illumines all the same
city of no possession
city of the passing thought
this is the fourth season
when the living learn to sleep
and warm themselves and sing
how we depend
on one another
as a matter
of course
winter radiates
us forth

and so we close our eyes
across the bridge
if sleep has a color
it is the darkest blue
that lays beneath
the river's silver-
brass-bright skin
awake is the color
of dawn and the bridge
is the texture of work
intricately
hammered strings
that hold their taut
and fastening
through day-white cloud
blue sky each one of us
closes our eyes
across the bridge
the texture of the city
is the smooth chalk
bubble of brick
is the coarse black
of asphalt roof
is the fine high polish
of the new tower

with its foolish snout
stuck in the sky
like a rocket
the color of a dawn
we are always promised
but never see
and so we close our eyes

we fly apart
through the not-yet-dark
the broken parade down 5th
like broken toys
it is almost thanksgiving
and the buildings are looking
through their glasses
as we blur right by
a sleight of hand
it is not grace that opens
to let us burrow in
it's a chaos of reordering
which of these
is the obstacle
to understanding
how the magic happens
we stop each other
from certain transgressions
by looking very directly
to say *I see you*
is to admit
this impediment
there is a point
right before
the DeKalb stop

when we two trains
are hip to hip
and then we fly apart

we barrel forwards
long heads nodding
spring splitting open
the cloud-dark sky
and letting all the light in
and letting all the people out
the seasons are all con men
we have never seen before
but the lens clouds
the window frosts
so the light looks
like we know it
even though it offers
such other
moorings
we store up
our Sundays
shore up our flood gates
til the hammer cracks
and the shoot flies open
full of animal pain
try and a dream
of the weirdest
kind of glory
to stay on

this maniacal ride
longer than anyone
we barrel forwards

we fall

are reared

into the day

as shapes this bright

container can contain

among the white

swift moving lights

that hem the city in

the other bridge

holds out her arms

two tired

and tireless women

working through the night

to usher us across

this is how

we fall back in

to be reared into day

we stand beside each other
and tightly hold our stories
the buildings face us
we face the other bridge
and the water faces the sky
we hold our breath
and dive into
the thousands
of windows
of Chinatown
of the Lower East Side
the immigrants arrive
and we navigate
that difference
allows for us to face
each stark and present all
a torrent of fall and glory
to stand beside
each other and tightly hold
our stories

if this animation were suspended
each piece could be erased
til we were only these
rushing bodies without river
bridge or train we might stop
mid-lurch in the moment
before gravity
removes the foolish lines
we draw around our edges
the pink sky at 8:13 AM returns
and the rest of the city rushes in
until our animation is suspended

among the shore's

grey soot and tar

are numbers carved

against redaction

monuments ghosting

the ground like those

pulled from

the southern end

ghost the sky

in which the stars

inviolately sigh

church bells find us

high and low

until we count

ourselves among

the furniture

of their green yards

along the shore's

grey soot and tar

we are the moviegoers
faces lit
against a darkening sky
a sea of us
at 6:24 PM
look onto the
already night
that's gathered up its ink
and billows toward us
like a squid
all cloud and tentacles
this day
receding into night
this posse
of black coats aloft
in a plume of dust
we're a fist
full of dynamite
the waterfront
Chinatown
the subways rife
with warriors
dark-eyed orphans
watching each other
through the windows

of the passing train
we can finally
watch each other
safely encased
in frames of light
we moviegoers
aflame onscreen
in the darkening night

to persist through sleep

we hunker forth

vibrate across

the skeletal harp

rib cage folded hands

squat atlas spanned

across the gun-grey

river rocks

into an island

wild with giant

gun-grey trees

we and the grey

persistent trees

leap forth

to live

through sleep

the red heart beats
its light and we
are blurred right by
each push across
the bridge is one
more time we have
not met release
lit windows
adumbrate
at 6:00 PM
what else
a teenager swears
aliens *exist*
her friend demurs
what else
we move against
is the almost-stall
at winter's door
enrobed and poor
in the redblack night
that beats its heart
into the blurring light

in winter there is
no tender earth
we slog across
the bridge of no
volition of our own
agraria is fast asleep
trees in their smooth bark
and winter's grip has fastened us
but only to a dumb routine
the sun appears innocently
because the sun is innocent
phenomena with no intent
a steady path whose length
is not to understand
we trick ourselves
across the bridge
one comfort's worth
another's loss
the empty firepits retreat
into imaginary dark
as though there were
no tender earth

the city recedes into mist

snow fails to mark the ground

but wraps her ghostly arms around

Manhattan's proud tall spires

a tiny boat is moored

just off the shore

the city drops

back into lore

it is 9:32 AM

in the morning after

the machine age

left us

just enough to change us

so that we might never

be alone

so America

solicits the east

solicits the east

a throng of stopped cranes

noses an empty sky

there is a vibrancy

in pools of light

and this is not

nostalgia

it's a prism

radiating out

and the city recedes into mist

like disassembled birds
we hurtle through the sky
our bodies packed in feathers
and the trains rush past
a blur of yellow white
the river full of dark no sky
to speak of or reflect
warehouses yawn
with empty lit-up heads
where brains would be
if buildings know
how to be in one place
for a hundred years
how do they
address us
blurring past
our coats and packages
our soft and tender bodies
our fitted shoes and pants
we are like packages
of moving parts
how we hurtle
through the sky
like disassembled birds

air's splinter
we are sway
we meet the
telegraphic day
collective hearts
on foot lean toward
the city like a pack
of cards or crop of wheat
planting ourselves
in air like spores
into the blue
the color of
the bridge
a metal sky
whorled hush of fat
white clouds we push
across the bridge
our burdens snug
on backs our tongues
in languages
a tugboat tugs
its wake and tags
bloom elderly
recumbent trees
dropping their leaves

in hopes of splintering
and we the dry
percussive flowers
in the gale we are
for sway

having listened
to warnings
about strangers
the train pulls us into
the sky like a seabed
we close our clamshells
to filter out the grit
until the morning
spat between lovers
enters like someone
else's pearl and we turn
our eyes to the wide
open windows
and open our hands
and our feet and our
foreheads to the current
of everyone in the train's
almost aerodynastic rush
as she leaps into the loud
impossible dark
having lit up
the tunnel's opening maw
having listened

if we are struggling

over the bridge

then we are at

our worst or best

thus this

polemic sway

the river

absolutely blue

and liberty

absolutely green

the bridge is one

of many binding

the city to the earth

unfinished buildings

reveal their skeletons

everybody needs

an antagonist

says the man

in the green wool

hat his laughter

the color of trees

against the white noise

of the subway roll

if all we hear is laughter

if all we hear is noise

if we are struggling

agglomerated frozen stars
ornament the bridge
we have come to this
history
talking to itself
reluctant guest
agglomeration of fire
and stars articulating
themselves frozen
and apart

across the bridge
we sleep the sleep
of the blue-white sheet
reflecting mute
bright power
to illumine
not to alter shape
but usher in
the eye's purview
a radiance
illuminates
aluminum can trains
slugging across
its latticework applied
a plie held apart
the bridge resembles nothing
so much as we resemble
each other plugging in
to a remembered dark
"I love Javier"
"I love. . . "
blue smear of ink
so florid
in the halogenic light
we sleep inside
across the bridge

gravity's thrall
pins us to motion
the train shakes
its gravitron
in the embrace
of music's offer
of another all
our necks bend
like metal birds
in the West
Texas desert
we pull our eyes
very closed
like singers
in the fold
of a hymn thrummed
of a string plucked
of anything flung
into gravity's thrall

it's a kind of sympathy
a slumber we allow
to roll over us
like a long
tired sound
a scrim
of forgetting
there are seldom barbs
where the rails ride
very straight
even air
has its inclement
hurdles
its parting fat clouds
static lighting up
their cheeks
with a kind
of sympathy

packed in together
it is easy to feel
like a vessel of blood
in a warm-dark tunnel
only once have I traveled
at the same speed
as the train across the bridge
so that a man's face
turned toward the window
was foreground to the swift
obliterating city
that glowed abstractly behind him
it's not nostalgic
to suddenly love
my neighbor across the bridge
it's not sentiment
that allows my body
to rest in the orange bench
while my neighbor blurs
his beaten drum
and ducks beneath
the passive air
we are packed in together

to arc

to over

reach then

come back

into comfort

of flight

presumes

a narrow path

togetherness

is rich talk

we count up

these coins of

by ourselves

then reach

to arc

we forget our way
across the bridge
possessed by trains
fed and reared
by anonymous crowds
the bridge with her shock
of yellow-white sky
and the specter of water
is gracious enough
to let us forget
all of history
we ride a black sound
into a bright day
a voltage of wind
like a heavy thing
being dragged across
a heavier thing
the man standing
tilts his head
posing for a close-up
the bridge is a spiral
staircase of ash
we do not deny
that we push
on the bridge

as the bridge
pushes us
through the bright day
with a black sound
she hands her dumb
and dreaming children
to bright blank air
we need no baptism
to ogle
an expanse of land
a streak of shore
to forget everything
we live for
is to carry inside us
an ocean of salt
and this is how
the bridge pulls us
through the sky:
we forget our way
across the bridge
across the bridge
across the bridge

the difference
between if and so
is the same line
between sky and snow
the air charges
with push and or
the trucks swarm
the streets to take
apart the storm
the river is
awake and frilled
with arctic
and exotic lace
a lone tug stopped
in the river's embrace
considers the flag
flapping like a fish
at the top of the bridge
we tug and are tugged
into the residue
of weather into
the difference

we're all impressing
our light on some highly
sensitive surface this
delirious morning
the river enormous
even the most
violent bodies
of water exert
a calming effect
and so with air
move with the wind
as with a hundred
passengers
among whom our
own bodies sit
and strangeness
blankets the crowd
like an impressive snow

we have chosen this
unglamorous
mechanical lullaby
wrapped in a shawl
of concrete and light
it is 7:09 PM
for all the Poles
Chinese and French
who sway like a stall
of ponies staring
away the afternoon
to stand unvarnished
in the barely dark
of the dinner hour
together and alone
as stalled small horses
is what we have chosen

only fog
at 9:15 AM
white cloud and yellow
taxi on the bridge

there is no guarantee
across the bridge
no formal agreement
if we were made
to fall today
the river would receive us
as she receives her rust
and pitch colored barges
piers dipped in light
fishes orderly in the wake
of proud small trans-
atlantic tugs
to live in a city
that will never be lost
is to write ourselves
indelibly in
to the tenor of travel
the rasp of its wake
it is Tuesday 8:42 AM
and winter is wet
and falling from the sky
the street is grand
and blue in this
late morning hour
of no guarantee

we have no gifts
but the bright shock of sun
and the leaves lying just
beneath the silvery
bark of trees
the river says
nothing today
her mouth of rain
and the browning sludge
of her private retreats
a ferocious turn
lands in the wake
of a haggard
filthy tug
so the rain stands
on all the roofs
at once until
the clouds let it all
back in
visibly this
economy
of sky
goes on
without purchase
or generosity

everything is used
and then transformed
for other use
we use each other
for safety threat
and speculation
in this way we
resemble clouds
and how we reside
very occasionally
in the sky
with no transactions
taking place
except what we take
with our rapacious eyes
from a sky
that offers
unspeakable blue
we have no word for
radiant gift
this sunlight
charging up the sky

because we can't be fixed
we perform ourselves
across the bridge
the moon performs its swing
cheshiring over
the red black yellow
of the moving
and the unmoved
thoroughfares
at most
at rest unable
to do anything
but listen and pour
at 10:15 PM
over TVs glowing
blue in the black
of the night
where we sometimes
shortly sigh
gasp sing a little
these performances
are these moved populace
because we can't be fixed

the night is about
to fill with snow
so we roll through
the premonition
before the storm
the city dresses
elegantly in black
with her wide open
windows
she'll drape in white
til white and dark
are stacked like the scarf
of the blackhaired woman
in black reading a black
book and holding on
to evening (it's 7:13)
with three fingers
the days are getting
longer but right
now the night's
about to start

not without sun

or joy are we

pushed into day

as a rill of cool

air pulls into

a sleeper's mouth

parting

as the river parts

to follow white

gulls black birds and

the vessels which

have borne our most

dogged tries

so we fill our cities

with more try until

we have demanded

everything

impossible

is not without sun

or joy

if the bridge
is a pillar of salt
the flag is a gun
made of doves
lenticular print
observing the crowd
so if we become
another lenticular
that moves between
watching and singing
together we'll make
a geometry
we can all
agree on
it will stand
like a table
each leg carrying
its own weight:
one threat
one ideal
one pillar of salt

to question the existence
of the bridge is to pull
each fraying thread
from the raveling cloth
everything falls apart
the congress of fishes
the redwhite cars
the electrical plant
even the man so buried
beneath his hat
I will not remember
his face even though
he is here in this book
because to question
that the man
hides his real
living face
beneath a short brim
of black wool
or the sodium lights
flaring beneath
the unimaginable bridge
is to question the churn
and thrum of my own

selfish heart
too convinced
of its own right
to question

having knit ourselves
to winter's frost
having drummed this salt
air til we could
no longer rise
what happens now
that this bridge carries
us the same
as those that cover
other rivers?
each of these
preposterous
monstrosities bequeathed
in dream and the cold
dark salt of work
delivers its payload
to a changed
and changing earth
this train we ride
is relic and harbinger
at once we must
live closer
having knit ourselves
to winter's frost

a woman goes over a bridge
a man walks through
a changing crowd
a shaft of light
and then his shadow
joins the shade
of 10 AM still
morning in this
altering state
whose colors
I have made
a morning song
a comfort where
each pillar of salt
falls into finer
particles smaller
lush and forever
as prairie this perspective
crystalline and meant
to be as monumental
as the dance of death
in the yawn of the west
in the jaws of the east so
we join our rivers so

the adolescent throng
awakes a changed
and changing crowd
the brackish water
churns and churns
a bullet fills a barrel
a man rides a cataract
a woman goes over a bridge

at the end
of the zoetrope
between DeKalb
and the bridge
the rocket takes off
and disappears
fires back and crowds
out everything orderly
the trees green
roofs a chaos of paint
the ants along the BQE
the zoetrope
returns us
to our beginnings
as to our endings—
the rocket firing back

the window opens only
to a rush of wind
we glance only once
at one another
because the train
is a house
built of sticks
each of us
load-bearing beams
so careful our tinder
and pointed our rest
we deserve to share this
junk-scarred outpost
this cyclone of seasons
I'd like to know what
exactly is American
about me a map
of my neural pathways
a list of my most
charged associations
I know at least
how strange is the
American train
pulling passengers
into the sky

like a net of silver
flashing fish
and a flare of sun
moves behind the city
because it is tired and done
this is not very American
but it is American
this train is a house
with its doors thrown
open only
to a rush of wind

if sunlight could fill our bellies
it would weigh like salt water
the clouds would simmer off
til the sky was a blue
true dream of satisfied
yes this is the birth
of anatomies
unfettered by error
relieved to be nothing
but their very own shape
some of us are bells
some root and make earth
some fall all over
the three-colored ground
exploring the horror
of governance
entropy
and grace
that we say
like a chant
help us help us help us
fill our bellies with the sun

ACKNOWLEDGMENTS

25 poems in this manuscript appeared as a limited edition chapbook of 100 copies entitled *The Bridge*, released by Push Press in 2011.

Heartfelt thanks to Jay Grabowski and Jason Morris of Push Press for their instigating belief and work for this book, and to the editors of the following journals in which pieces of *The Bridge* appeared: *Mrs. Maybe, Portable Boog City 2011, 20012, Big Bell, Boog City Festival Reader, Bright Pink Mosquito, High Chair, LyreLyre, Boston Review, Lungfull!, Pinwheel, Amerarcana: A Bird & Beckett Review*, and *Forklift, Ohio*.

Enduring gratitude to Joseph Massey for his tremendously generous interest in making this book's publication possible, to Tony Frazer for his confidence in *The Bridge* and the gift of his time, to Paula Cisewski and Kyle Dargan for their kind and responsive blessings, and to my parents for their great love of books and language.

I am most deeply grateful to Chris Martin, whose daily devotion to poetry inspired the habit that produced these poems, and for his unflagging support of my work.

Mary Austin Speaker is a poet and book designer.
The author of *Ceremony*, which was selected
by Matthea Harvey as winner of the 2013 Slope
Editions poetry prize, she has also published four
chapbooks, including *The Bridge* (Push Press
2011) and *20 Love Poems for 10 Months* (Ugly
Duckling Presse 2012) and a collaborative play,
I Am You This Morning You Are Me Tonight,
written with her husband, the poet Chris Martin.
She lives in Minneapolis.

CPSIA information can be obtained at www.ICGtesting.com
Printed in the USA
LVOW07s1959201215

466702LV00002B/22/P